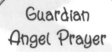

Guardian Angel Prayer

Angel of God,
my Guardian dear
to whom God's love
commits me here.
Ever this day
be at my side
to light and guard
to rule and guide.
Amen.

My
Guardian Angel
Prayer Book

Is a Gift to

_____

Given with love from

_____

On the occasion of

_____

on

_____

Guardian Angel
Prayer Book

Guardian Angel Prayer Book

Written and Edited by
Rev. Victor Hoagland, C. P.

Illustrated by
Samuel J. Butcher

Regina Press
New York

THE REGINA PRESS
10 Hub Drive
Melville, New York

My Dear Child:

Guardian Angels are a sign of God's love and care for you and every child in all the world.

This small, first book of prayers has been given to you by someone who also loves and cares for you very much.

As you grow and learn the meanings of these beautiful prayers, may God's love always hold you close to Jesus' heart.

Fr. Victor

The Sign of the Cross

In the name of the Father,
and of the Son,
and of the Holy Spirit. Amen.

Glory Be

Glory be to the Father
and to the Son
and the Holy Spirit,
as it was in the beginning,
is now and ever shall be,
world without end. Amen.

Grace Before Meals

Bless us, O Lord, and these Your gifts
which we are about to receive
from Your bounty
Through Christ our Lord. Amen.

Grace After Meals

We give you thanks, O almighty God,
for all your benefits;
You who live and reign,
world without end. Amen.

The Our Father

Our Father, who art in heaven,
hallowed be Thy name,
Thy kingdom come,
Thy will be done,
on earth as it is in heaven.
Give us this day our daily bread,
and forgive us our trespasses
as we forgive those
who trespass against us,
and lead us not into temptation,
but deliver us from evil. Amen.

The Hail Mary

Hail Mary, full of grace,
the Lord is with thee;
blessed art thou among women,
and blessed is the fruit
of thy womb, Jesus.
Holy Mary, Mother of God,
pray for us sinners now
and at the hour of our death. Amen.

Guardian Angel Prayer

Angel of God
my Guardian dear
to whom God's love
commits me here.
Ever this day
be at my side
to light and guard
to rule and guide. Amen.

The Chief Spiritual Works of Mercy

To admonish the sinner.

To instruct the ignorant.

To counsel the doubtful.

To comfort the sorrowful.

To bear wrongs patiently.

To forgive all injuries.

To pray for the living
and the dead.

The Chief Corporal
Works of Mercy

To feed the hungry.

To give drink to the thirsty.

To clothe the naked.

To visit the imprisoned.

To shelter the homeless.

To visit the sick.

To bury the dead.

The Sacraments

1. Baptism

2. Reconciliation

3. Holy Eucharist

4. Confirmation

5. Anointing of the Sick

6. Holy Orders

7. Matrimony

The Beatitudes

1. Blessed are the poor in spirit, for the kingdom of heaven is theirs.

2. Blessed are those who are sad, for they shall be comforted.

3. Blessed are the mild and gentle, for they shall inherit the land.

4. Blessed are those who hunger and thirst for justice, for they shall be filled.

5. Blessed are the merciful, for they shall receive mercy.

6. Blessed are the pure in heart, for they shall see God.

7. Blessed are those who make peace, for they shall be called the children of God.

8. Blessed are those who suffer for my sake, for heaven will be theirs.

The Ten Commandments

1. I, the Lord, am your God. You shall not have other gods besides me.
2. You shall not take the name of the Lord, your God, in vain.
3. Remember to keep holy the sabbath day.
4. Honor your father and your mother.
5. You shall not kill.
6. You shall not commit adultery.
7. You shall not steal.
8. You shall not bear false witness against your neighbor.
9. You shall not covet your neighbor's wife.
10. You shall not covet anything that belongs to your neighbor.

The Rosary

The Joyful Mysteries

1. The Coming of Jesus is Announced
2. Mary Visits Elizabeth
3. Jesus is Born
4. Jesus is Presented to God
5. Jesus is Found in the Temple

The Sorrowful Mysteries

1. Jesus' Agony in the Garden
2. Jesus is Whipped
3. Jesus is Crowned with Thorns
4. Jesus Carries His Cross
5. Jesus Dies on the Cross

The Glorious Mysteries

1. Jesus Rises from His Tomb
2. Jesus Ascends to Heaven
3. The Holy Spirit Descends
4. Mary is Assumed into Heaven
5. Mary is Crowned in Heaven